lost dreams

t. kilgore splake
25214 ash street
calumet, mi 49913
splake@chartermi.net

transcendent zero press
houston, tx
www.transcendentzeropress.org

PUBLISHED BY TRANSCENDENT ZERO PRESS
www.transcendentzeropress.org

ISBN-13: 978-1-946460-99-8
ISBN-10: 1-946460-99-0

Printed in the United States of America

Transcendent Zero Press
16429 El Camino Real Apt. 7
Houston, TX 77062

FIRST EDITION

dead poet's organizer
collections of mad desires
waiting waiting waiting

some of the poems in "lost dreams" and been previously published in the literary journals "brevities," in california, and "bear creek haiku" in colorado.

BRIEF OPENING NOTE
Dustin Pickering, Publisher

splake confided in me that he felt this work is his best to date. I won't judge quality as par with splake's quantity; that is, let's wait before we cast any stones.

And speaking of stones, how's the creek splake?

These works bear a sense of finality, of life's lusts left to the page and the poet's immortality born for the world of appearance. Everything must be recorded for ETERNITY! There are no words worth their smiles without eternity. Masks could not be held by the thumb and forefinger without some deep, dark mystery.

Where does this come into splake's work? Perhaps the 'lost dreams' are actually sacrifices made to immortalize one's self, one's aches as the poet has done here. Or perhaps the 'lost dreams' are what underlies our base world of appearance. splake, in his usual idiosyncratic way, explores the boundary between dream and reality.

Is reality indeed a lost dream? Is there something more to life than the tepid uncertainties we are filled with, the overbearing joys, the lusts and visions, the purpose we grant ourselves?

The pond is an appearance; though being a pond, it hides much, it sustains. Waters flow to the seas but we imagine little of such majesty. Dare an ill-reflected life reveal the hidden dream we are experiencing.

Is this also a lost dream?

thelonious monk
soft jazzy touch
world full of edges

movie theater screen
brief afternoon hours
young wild free

tornado yellow sky
calm before storm
poet's first word

cool oily kiss
thundering red explosion
poems covering trees

brain death hangover
cigarette nicotine hit
coffee melting phlegm

fifties childhood
living in black and white
today blinded by color

licking wet leaves
delicious morning dew
like emily drunk on air

poet's inheritance
stacks of small notebooks
years of failed dreams

artistic pretender
deeply insecure
needing someone's god

wannabe poet rising
stair-master success
floor after imaginary floor

pretty girl cheap beer
taking standing eight-count
not wanting more

girl raised special person
now middle-aged woman
lying to herself

woman's beauty products
like wine-wafer celebration
reason to believe

love making distractions
counting orgasms
feeling none

imagining love making
loose tight wet dry
too too too

mad depressive suffering
seeking therapist help
fitting back in tiny box

whores and fours
no poker pot
arthritic hands can't shuffle

walking over tiny lives
things eyes can't see
waiting to inherit earth

marrying fourth wife
domineering cunt ball buster
waiting new pain

30 days in rehab
regular aa meetings
repeating others' words

empty jack daniels bottle
leonard cohen voice fading
solar eclipse blackout

solitary hiker
quiet space for thinking
without four putt green

uniformed policy authority
belt holstered gun
scarecrow able to kill

labor day freedom
diane arbus tourist friends
returning to their zoo

loud phony rebel
unappreciated genius
first to sell out

early first light
black soul rising
soon touching heaven

tampax
bottle of advil
icy tall boy

patti smith loud
deafening angry resentment
baby due next week

diamond on finger
ignoring mother's advice
watching computer porn

plain white underwear
dreams of satin bikini
black lacy thong

circus center ring star
clown lion tamer acrobat
poet shoveling shit

phone batteries dead
consciousness disappearing
life no longer exists

life deafening explosion
jackson pollock t-shirt
red splattered art

chalking cue tip
pool balls clicking
green felt pulse

poet ashes scattered
remote stream waters
feeding rainbow souls

writing day reflections
like movie final credits
theater still dark

after last call
musicians warming up
electricity in the air

life brief
not dying before
leaving starlight smear

searching wilderness shadows
like monk circling cloister
quietly seeking wisdom

lost in cold whiteness
wind driven snow
poet drunk on silence

becoming housewife
cooking laundry shopping
whispering headache

failed poet
discovering new talent
criticizing others

disappearing through crack
beyond mirror reflection
itch of naked flesh

daily diary entries
notes to myself
inventing another life

power of words
stripping away illusions
leaving painful reality

existential crisis
graying poets dying
newborns not ready

writer's block
playing russian roulette
all chambers empty

solitary heron silhouette
evening marsh shadows
naked zen

northern v circling
waiting god's decision
formation leaving south

imaginary mountain man
reading survival books
empty wilderness dreams

black angry clouds
last autumn leaves
clinging in wind

breast bombs
feminine cojones cred
i am woman

fiery lightning flashes
burning through mirror
poet's brain on fire

pinball replay wizard
blinking lights lots of flippers
no balls in machine

free enterprise genius
unless you wear a beard
write black beret poetry

run to daylight
on the road escape
poet going home

driving with headlights off
like drunken moth
navigating by moon light

quiet moment passing
calm of insanity
or existential bliss

lifetime belongings
years of impulse buying
citizen of qvc and ebay

golden retirement years
between doctors appointments
x-rays and tests

ymca poker dollars
whores and fours wild
playing bus fare home

jogger's earplug tight
loud music drowning
new ideas in brain

worn blue jeans
denim caressing soft ass
ecstasy waiting escape

morning contesting muse
quiet coffee shop corner
espresso words exploding

computer porn
showing cocks and pussies
no hearts or brains

penis inside pussy
house wife children
ecstasy into madness

religion denying sex
shaming naked body
sad paradise lost

sin guilt shame
punishing children's lives
growing up afraid

rolling thunder flashing lightning
fierce storm's approach
poems whispering in winds

following dangerous hunt
describing successful kill
sharpened bone and blood

standing in arctic chill
rain stinging face
lost in memories

magnum chambered round
clock stuck on four-thirty
trout stream slowly vanishing

continuously arranging tools
pieces of his life
no longer working

cliffs and brautigan creek
keweenaw my tibet
lost horizons home

poet's ashes scattered
light wilderness breeze
sky taking him home

www.ingramcontent.com/pod-product-compliance
Lightning Source LLC
Chambersburg PA
CBHW071450040426
42445CB00012BA/1508